Soccer ★ ★ ★ Stars

George Ivanoff

Soccer Stars

Text: George Ivanoff
Publishers: Tania Mazzeo and Eliza Webb
Series consultant: Amanda Sutera
  Hands on Heads Consulting
Editor: Sarah Layton
Project editor: Annabel Smith
Designer: Leigh Ashforth
Project designer: Danielle Maccarone
Permissions researchers: Corrina Gilbert and Liz McShane
Production controller: Renee Tome

Acknowledgements
We would like to thank the following for permission to reproduce copyright material:

Front cover, p. 23 (background): Adobe Stock/LeArchitecto; front cover (top left), pp. 14, 19, 23 (centre): Alamy Stock Photo/Trinity Mirror/Mirrorpix; front cover (top right), pp. 16, 23 (bottom right): Alamy Stock Photo/Jonathan Larsen/Diadem Images; front cover (bottom left), pp. 6, 23 (top left): Alamy Stock Photo/ZUMA Press Inc; front cover (bottom middle), pp. 8, 13, 23 (top middle): Alamy Stock Photo/Action Plus Sports Images; front cover (bottom right), pp. 10, 23 (middle left): Alamy Stock Photo/Anthony Devlin Photography; pp. 1, 4, 6, 9, 11, 13, 15, 17, 19, 21, 24, back cover (soccer ball): Shutterstock.com/ irin-k; p. 4: iStock.com/fotokostic; pp. 5, 12, 23 (top right): Alamy Stock Photo/Sipa USA; p. 7 (main): Alamy Stock Photo/UK Sport Pics Ltd; p. 9 (main): Getty Images/Matt King/Stringer; p. 11 (main): Getty Images/ Gualter Fatia/Contributor; p. 15 (main): Getty Images/Tom Purslow; p. 17 (main): Alamy Stock Photo/Aflo Co., Ltd.; pp. 18, 21 (main), 23 (bottom left): Alamy Stock Photo/PA Images; pp. 20, 23 (bottom middle): Alamy Stock Photo/PCN Photography; p. 22: iStock.com/ FatCamera.

Every effort has been made to trace and acknowledge copyright. However, if any infringement has occurred, the publishers tender their apologies and invite the copyright holders to contact them.

NovaStar

Text © 2024 Cengage Learning Australia Pty Limited

ISBN 978 0 17 033392 4

Cengage Learning Australia
Level 5, 80 Dorcas Street
Southbank VIC 3006 Australia
Phone: 1300 790 853
Email: aust.nelsonprimary@cengage.com

For learning solutions, visit **cengage.com.au**

Printed in China by 1010 Printing International Ltd
1 2 3 4 5 6 7 28 27 26 25 24

Nelson acknowledges the Traditional Owners and Custodians of the lands of all First Nations Peoples. We pay respect to Elders past and present, and extend that respect to all First Nations Peoples today.

Contents

Super Soccer   4

Soccer Stars from Around the World   6

  Samantha Kerr   6

  Tim Cahill   8

  Cristiano Ronaldo   10

  Lionel Messi   12

  David Beckham   14

  Homare Sawa   16

  Diego Maradona   18

  Pelé   20

Be a Soccer Star!   22

Glossary   24

Index   24

Super Soccer

Soccer is a sport that is loved by many people. It is played in most countries around the world.

A game of soccer is played between two teams, each with 11 players. The aim of the game is to score the most goals by kicking a ball into the other team's goal. Unlike other football games, players in soccer must not touch the ball with their hands.

In most places, the game of soccer is just called "football". In countries where other types of football are played, it is called "soccer".

In soccer, players control the ball using their feet, knees and legs.

Lots of people play soccer for fun.
But some players are **professionals**.
Read on to find out about some of the greatest
soccer stars to ever play the game!

Lydia Williams plays soccer for the Australian
women's national team, the Matildas.

Soccer Stars from Around the World

Samantha Kerr

NAME → Samantha Kerr

DATE OF BIRTH → 10 September 1993

COUNTRY OF BIRTH → Australia

Samantha Kerr is known as one of the world's best soccer **strikers**.

Samantha Kerr appears in the popular video game *FIFA 23 Ultimate Edition.*

★ Samantha Kerr started her professional **career** at the age of 15 with the Perth Glory soccer club in Australia.

★ Kerr has been captain of the Australian women's national soccer team, the Matildas, since 2019.

★ By the end of the FIFA Women's World Cup in 2023, Kerr had scored 64 goals in international games. This makes her Australia's highest international goalscorer.

Samantha Kerr scores a goal against England in the FIFA Women's World Cup in 2023.

Tim Cahill

NAME → Tim Cahill

NICKNAME → Tiny Tim

DATE OF BIRTH → 6 December 1979

COUNTRY OF BIRTH → Australia

Tim Cahill is famous for his "heading", or his ability to hit the ball with his head rather than kicking it.

FAST FACTS

★ Tim Cahill played for teams in Australia, England, the USA, India and China.

★ In 2006, Cahill became the first Australian to ever score a goal in a FIFA World Cup match.

★ Cahill holds the record for the most goals scored in a World Cup match by an Australian – five!

Tim Cahill heads the ball to score a goal for the Australian men's national team, the Socceroos, in 2018.

After scoring a goal, Tim Cahill often celebrated by punching one of the flags that marked the corners of the pitch.

Cristiano
Ronaldo

NAME → Cristiano Ronaldo dos Santos Aveiro

NICKNAME → CR7 (Cristiano Ronaldo, plus the number he has worn the most in his career – 7)

DATE OF BIRTH → 5 February 1985

COUNTRY OF BIRTH → Portugal

Cristiano Ronaldo is world-famous for his footwork, or the way he controls the soccer ball with his feet.

FAST FACTS

★ Cristiano Ronaldo has played for teams in Portugal, England, Spain and Italy.

★ Ronaldo has played in over 1100 soccer matches and scored over 800 goals.

★ Ronaldo has won 32 trophies and many awards.

Cristiano Ronaldo moves the ball forward in a Portugal World Cup match in 2006.

Cristiano Ronaldo has an airport named after him in Portugal.

Lionel
Messi

PLAYER PROFILE

NAME → Lionel Messi

NICKNAME → The Atomic Flea

DATE OF BIRTH → 24 June 1987

COUNTRY OF BIRTH → Argentina

Lionel Messi is famous for being one of the most highly skilled soccer players of all time.

FAST FACTS

★ Lionel Messi spent most of his career at Spain's Barcelona Football Club (FC Barcelona). He changed teams in 2021 to join the Paris Saint-Germain Football Club in France.

★ Messi is FC Barcelona's all-time top goalscorer, with 672 goals.

★ Messi has won the European Golden Shoe award (given to the highest goalscorer each year) six times – more than any other player.

Lionel Messi has cousins who are professional soccer players, and his dad is a **coach**. At age five, Lionel joined the team his dad coached.

Lionel Messi plays for Argentina in a World Cup match in 2022.

David
Beckham

David Beckham is known for having one of the best kicks in the game of soccer. He could kick the ball so that it would curve (or bend) as it moved through the air.

FAST FACTS

★ David Beckham spent most of his career playing for the English team Manchester United, but he has also played for teams in Spain, the USA, Italy and France.

★ Beckham played for the English national team from 1996 to 2009. He was the captain of the team from 2000 to 2006.

David Beckham is married to Victoria Beckham, who was once in the pop group, the Spice Girls.

David Beckham plays in a "Legends" game for the English team Manchester United in 2019.

Homare
Sawa

NAME → Homare Sawa

DATE OF BIRTH → 6 September 1978

COUNTRY OF BIRTH → Japan

Homare (say: *ho-mah-reh*) Sawa is known as one of the greatest soccer players in Asia.

FAST FACTS

★ Homare Sawa played soccer for teams in Japan and the USA.

★ She was captain of the Japanese national team when they won the FIFA Women's World Cup in 2011 and an Olympic silver medal at the London Olympic Games in 2012.

★ Homare won the FIFA Women's World Player of the Year award in 2011.

Homare Sawa plays for Japan at the Beijing Olympic Games in 2008.

Homare Sawa began playing soccer when she was only six years old.

Diego
Maradona

NAME → Diego Maradona

NICKNAME → The Golden Boy

DATE OF BIRTH → 30 October 1960

COUNTRY OF BIRTH → Argentina

Diego Maradona, one of the most famous soccer players in the world, was known for his ball skills and his ability to **weave** and dodge between opposing players.

FAST FACTS

★ Diego Maradona played for teams in Argentina, Spain and Italy.

★ Maradona was joint winner of the FIFA Player of the Twentieth Century award.

★ After Maradona **retired** from playing, he became a coach and **manager**. Maradona remained a coach until his death in 2020 at the age of 60.

Diego Maradona weaves between players in a 1982 World Cup match for Argentina.

Diego Maradona always trained with his shoelaces undone. He would only lace up his shoes when playing proper games.

Pelé

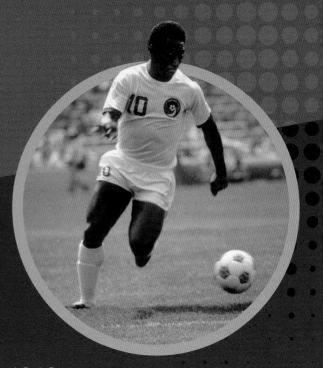

NAME → Edson Arantes do Nascimento

NICKNAME → Pelé

DATE OF BIRTH → 23 October 1940

COUNTRY OF BIRTH → Brazil

Edson Arantes do Nascimento is known to most people around the world by his nickname, Pelé. He is one of the most **successful** and popular sportspeople of all time.

FAST FACTS

★ Pelé began playing for Brazil's Santos Football Club at the age of 15. He also played for Brazil's national team.

★ Pelé is the all-time highest goalscorer for Brazil, with 77 goals in just 92 games.

★ Alongside Maradona, Pele was joint winner of the FIFA Player of the Twentieth Century award.

Pelé plays for the New York Cosmos in 1975.

When he was growing up, Pelé's family was very poor and couldn't afford a soccer ball. So, Pelé practised with a sock filled with newspaper.

Be a Soccer Star!

Soccer is one of the world's most popular sports, played by millions of people. Anyone can play! All you need is a ball and the willingness to learn. You, too, could become a soccer star!

To become a soccer star, the most important thing is to practise.

Samantha Kerr

Tim Cahill

Lionel Messi

Cristiano Ronaldo

David Beckham

Diego Maradona

Pelé

Homare Sawa

Glossary

career (*noun*)	the jobs a person does throughout their life
coach (*noun*)	the person who helps players train and improve their skills
manager (*noun*)	the head coach of a sports team
professionals (*noun*)	people who do something for money as a job
retired (*adjective*)	stopping the work you are doing, usually because you are getting older
strikers (*noun*)	players nearest to the opposing team's goal, whose job is to score as often as possible
successful (*adjective*)	doing very well at something
weave (*verb*)	to quickly change direction while running and dodging other people

Index

ball   **4, 8, 9, 10, 11, 14, 18, 21, 22**

Beckham, David   **14–15, 23**

Cahill, Tim   **8–9, 23**

career   **7, 12, 14, 24**

coach   **13, 18, 24**

FIFA   **7, 16, 18**

games   **4, 5, 6, 7, 14, 16, 17, 19, 20**

goals   **4, 7, 8, 9, 10, 12, 20, 24**

Kerr, Samantha   **6–7, 23**

Maradona, Diego   **18–19, 23**

Messi, Lionel   **12–13, 23**

Pelé   **20–21, 23**

players   **4, 5, 6, 8, 10, 12, 13, 14, 16, 18, 19, 20, 24**

Ronaldo, Cristiano   **10–11, 23**

Sawa, Homare   **16–17, 23**

sports   **4, 22, 24**

World Cup   **7, 8, 11, 13, 16, 19**